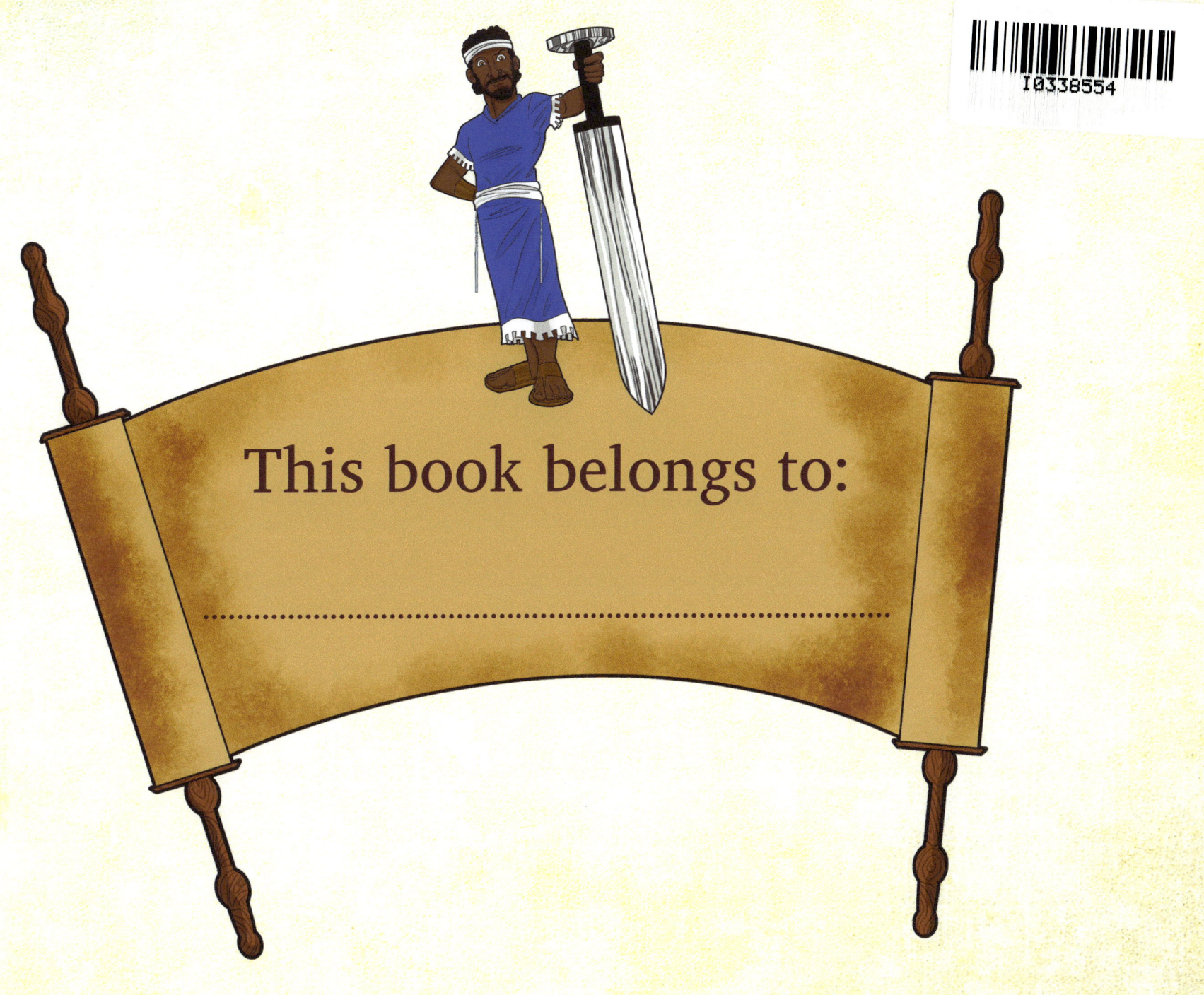

This book belongs to:

....

Copyright © BPA Publishing Ltd 2020

Author: Pip Reid
Illustrator: Thomas Barnett
Creative Director: Curtis Reid

www.biblepathwayadventures.com

Thank you for supporting Bible Pathway Adventures®. Our adventure series helps parents teach their children more about the Bible in a fun creative way. Designed for the whole family, Bible Pathway Adventures' mission is to help bring discipleship back into homes around the world. The search for truth is more fun than tradition!

The moral rights of author and illustrator have been asserted, this book is copyright.

ISBN: 978-0-473-38152-3

Facing the Giant

The adventures of David

"David took his staff in his hand and chose five smooth stones from the brook, and put them in his shepherd's pouch. His sling was in his hand..." (1 Samuel 17:40)

Do you need to be born into a royal family to be a king? Not when God is in charge! A long time ago, God chose a young shepherd named David from the tribe of Judah to become the king of Israel. God wanted to prove that He had picked the right man for the job. Before David became king, he faced many tests and had many exciting adventures.

Around this time, Israel was ruled by a disobedient king named Saul. With the help of his son Jonathan, Saul won many battles. But he stopped listening to God.

One day, Saul's army defeated a fierce enemy: the bloodthirsty Amalekites. Instead of destroying all of the people and animals like God had told him, Saul kept the best sheep and cattle for himself. "Save the king of Amalek," Saul said to his soldiers. "Let's keep him as our prisoner."

Did you know?

Many people believe there are different ways to pronounce God's name. These include Yah, Yahweh, Yahuah, and many others.

God was not pleased with Saul's bad behavior. He knew that if Saul saved the people and animals, the Amalekites would attack the Israelites again. He wanted obedience, so he spoke to His prophet Samuel.

"I am sorry that I made Saul king," God told Samuel. "He has turned away from Me and disobeyed My instructions. It is time for a new king of Israel." Samuel knew that God would take away the kingdom of Israel from Saul. He clasped his head in his hands and wept.

"Samuel, stop crying over Saul," said God. "Take some olive oil and go to Bethlehem. When you get there, find a man called Jesse. I have chosen one of his sons to be the new king."

Samuel was worried. "If Saul finds I'm looking for a new king, he'll kill me!" he said. Samuel may have been an important prophet, but Saul was still a powerful king. "Do not worry," said God. "Take a calf with you and say you have come to offer a sacrifice to Me. Invite Jesse to the meal. I will show you what to do next."

Samuel quickly obeyed God and hurried to Bethlehem. When he reached the gate of Bethlehem, the elders rushed out to greet him. "Why are you here?" they asked, their hands shaking. "Have you come in peace?" The elders had good reason to feel nervous. Samuel wasn't just a prophet; he was a judge and an army commander, too.

"Don't be afraid," Samuel told the men. "I'm here to offer a sacrifice to God. Come and join me." Samuel invited Jesse and his sons to the sacrifice, too. "God will choose the next king of Israel from among your sons," he told Jesse privately.

When Jesse and his sons arrived at the sacrifice, Samuel looked at Eliab, the oldest son. *Hmmm…this man is tall and handsome and looks like a king,* he thought. *He must be the man that God has chosen.*

But God had other ideas. "Ignore how handsome Eliab is," He said. "He is not the next king of Israel. I don't look at the outside of a person; I look at their heart."

One by one, Jesse brought his sons before Samuel. But each time, God said no. "God hasn't chosen any of these seven men," Samuel said to Jesse. "Do you have any other sons?" Jesse frowned and scratched his beard. "I have another son named David," he said. He pointed to a rocky hillside nearby where David was taking care of the sheep. "How could he be a king?"

Samuel peered at David through the window and smiled. He knew this was the man God had chosen to be the next king of Israel. "Tell him to come and see me," said Samuel, excitedly. "We will eat when he arrives."

Did you know?

Samuel was a Nazarite. This means he was set apart for God's service. Many biblical scholars believe this is why Samuel never cut his hair.
(1 Samuel 1:11)

David scrambled down the rocky path to meet Samuel. He was strong and handsome, with a twinkle in his eye. "Samuel, stand up and anoint him," said God. "He's the one!"

Samuel took his horn of olive oil and poured it carefully over David's head to show he would be the next king of Israel. Immediately, the Spirit of God came on David.

Jesse's sons looked at one another in surprise. Why had their youngest brother been anointed king and not one of them? But Samuel didn't give them any answers. His job was done. The people of Israel had their next king.

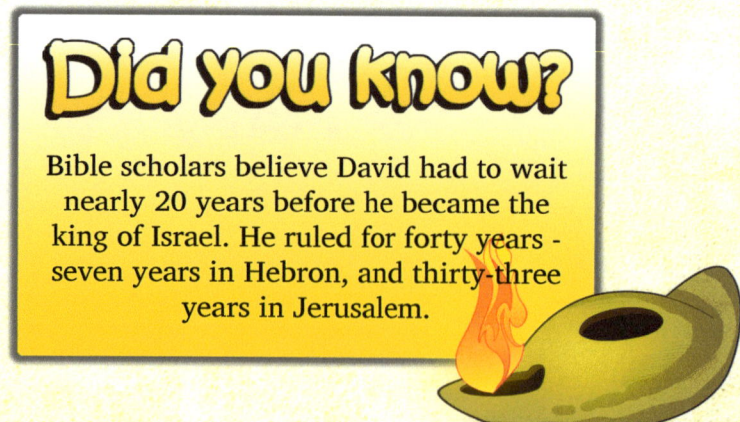

Did you know?

Bible scholars believe David had to wait nearly 20 years before he became the king of Israel. He ruled for forty years - seven years in Hebron, and thirty-three years in Jerusalem.

During this time, King Saul still ruled the land of Israel. He lived in a large stone palace in the town of Gibeah. Because he had been disobedient, the Spirit of God left him. Instead, an evil spirit entered the king and troubled him day and night. Nothing seemed to calm Saul's mind. His servants paced back and forth, wondering what to do.

"Let us find someone who can play the harp," they suggested. "Maybe the music will help you rest." Saul shrugged his shoulders and sighed. He didn't know why this evil spirit had come upon him.

"One of Jesse's sons in Bethlehem knows how to play the harp," said a servant. "He's a brave man who loves God. His name is David." King Saul liked the idea. He sent a message to Jesse, saying, "Send me your son David, the one who plays the harp."

Jesse sent David to the palace right away. After all, you couldn't disobey the king of Israel! And from that day on, whenever the evil spirit entered Saul, David sat beside the king and played his harp.

One day, the Israelites gathered together in the Elah Valley to fight their enemy, the fearsome Philistines. Nobody liked the Philistines much. They were wicked and cruel, and they liked a good fight.

King Saul glared across the valley at the Philistine army. They had lots of chariots and more soldiers than he could count. He grabbed his sword and quickly prepared for battle.

The king didn't know it yet, but the Philistines had a fearsome warrior on their side. His name was Goliath and he was as tall as a house! Everyone was afraid of him, and nobody came near him. Goliath was stronger than any man in the land of Israel.

Did you know?

During this era, there were no blacksmiths in the land of Israel. The Israelites took their iron tools to the Philistines to get sharpened. The Philistines charged a very high price for this service. (1 Samuel 13:20)

That afternoon, the Israelites lined up for battle against the Philistines. All of a sudden, a giant man marched out of the Philistine camp. It was the mighty giant, Goliath! He wore a bronze helmet on his head and a shiny breastplate made of bronze. Even his legs were covered in bronze armor so that no one could hurt him.

"Why are you here, you tiny Israelites?" roared Goliath. He flexed his bulging muscles. "If you dare, pick one of your men to fight me. If he wins, we will be your slaves, but if I win, you will be our slaves."

The Israelites shook with fear. They weren't used to fighting anyone as big as Goliath. Even the ground trembled when he walked. They stared at the giant, wide-eyed.

Meanwhile, in Bethlehem, Jesse told David to visit his three brothers who were soldiers in Saul's army. "Take these loaves of bread and go to the Elah Valley," he said. "Find out if your brothers are well, and then come back and tell me."

David wasted no time. The next morning, he jumped out of bed, took the sack of food, and set out to do as his father had ordered. He arrived at the camp, just as the soldiers were marching out to battle.

David dropped the sack of food on the ground and raced to the battle line to greet his brothers. He had never been so close to the enemy, and he was excited. He folded his arms and glared at the Philistines. How dare they try to destroy the Israelites!

"Why are you lined up for battle?" Goliath shouted to the Israelites. He had been threatening the Israelites for forty days, and he was growing impatient. "Come and fight me, you cowards!"

You would think the Israelites were used to hearing Goliath's threats, but they were even more frightened than before. They ran back to the camp as fast as their wobbly legs could carry them.

"That giant is a monster!" cried the soldiers. "If we could only kill him, we could get the reward the king promised!" David turned to the soldiers. "What's the reward for killing Goliath?" he asked. "Besides, who is this Philistine that dares to challenge the army of the living Elohim?"

Did you know?

Saul was 30 years old when he became the king of Israel. He reigned for 42 years.

The soldiers told David all about Goliath's challenge. Then, they told him what Saul had promised to the man who killed Goliath. "The king will give you his daughter to marry and will treat your family well," they said. David smiled. He liked the sound of the king's reward.

At that moment, David's brother Eliab stepped forward. "Why are you here, you wimp?" he said. He poked David in the chest with his spear. "You should be taking care of the sheep. You're not a warrior. You've only come to watch the fighting!"

"What have I done now?" asked David. He turned back to the soldiers. "I only asked a question." He ignored his older brother and continued talking with the men. In his heart, he wanted to help save the people of Israel from the Philistines.

When King Saul heard about David's bravery, he summoned David before him. "No one should be afraid of this Philistine!" David said to Saul. "I will go and fight him!"

"How can you fight this giant?" replied Saul. He looked David up and down, then shrugged. "Goliath is a great warrior and you're only a young boy."

"I have killed lions and bears to protect my father's sheep," said David. "God will help me kill this giant, too—just wait and see!" King Saul stroked his chin. He wasn't sure how to deal with Goliath. Could David be the answer?

Did you know?

King Saul was the tallest man in Israel. Some historians believe he was nearly seven feet tall.
(1 Samuel 9:2)

"Okay," King Saul finally said to David. "Go fight the giant, and may God be with you." He put a bronze helmet on David's head and gave him a coat of armor to wear.

David's heart pumped a little faster. He grabbed a sword and headed toward the battlefield. But he didn't get very far. "I can't wear all this armor! It's too big and heavy," he said. He ripped off the bronze helmet and gave the armor back to Saul. "Don't worry; I have another plan."

David knew that Goliath had four nasty sons. Holding his shepherd's stick, he picked five smooth stones from a nearby stream and put them in his pouch. Now he was ready for battle!

With his sling in his hand, David strolled towards Goliath. Goliath had waited for forty days, and he was ready to fight. "Am I a mad dog? Is that why you're carrying a stick?" said Goliath. "Why don't you Israelites give me a real soldier to fight?" David slowly twirled his empty sling and waited.

"Come closer," Goliath said to David. "I will give your body to the birds and animals to eat." David looked Goliath straight in the eye. "You come against me with a sword and a spear," he said. "But you don't scare me. I come against you in the name of God, the Elohim of this army."

Goliath nearly choked. How dare this Israelite boy threaten him? But David hadn't finished speaking. "God will hand you over to me! I'm going to kill you and give the bodies of the Philistines to the birds and animals," he said. "Then the whole world will know there is a God of Israel."

Did you know?

God often chose shepherds to lead the Hebrew people. Abraham, Isaac, Jacob, Moses, and David were all shepherds. Yeshua considered himself the 'good shepherd'.

Goliath had heard enough. Lifting his spear a little higher, he stomped toward David. Clouds of dust rose with each step the giant made, but David wasn't afraid. He took a stone from his bag, put it in his sling, and swung it three times above his head.

Whoosh! Whoosh! Whoosh!

David aimed the stone at the giant. It whizzed through the air like a rocket and smacked Goliath in the middle of his huge, hairy forehead. Goliath stumbled forward and crashed to the ground with a thud.

The Philistine soldiers stared at David in amazement. They could hardly believe the young shepherd had overpowered their great giant. David had beaten the mighty Philistine with just a sling and a stone!

David ran over to Goliath. "Now do you believe me?" he said. He pulled out the giant's sword and chopped off his head. The Israelite army let out a cheer. "God has given Goliath into our hands!" they shouted.

When the Philistines saw their hero was dead, they turned and ran away as fast as they could. But the Israelites didn't let them escape so easily. They picked up their weapons and chased the Philistine soldiers all the way back to their homes.

Did you know?

Giants (Nephilim) had six fingers on each hand and six toes on each foot.
(2 Sam 21:20 and 1 Chron 20:6)

David hadn't forgotten about Goliath's huge hairy head. He tucked it under his arm and carried it back to Jerusalem to show the king.

King Saul was pleased with David. "From now on, you work for me," he said. He placed a hand on David's shoulder. "You're a soldier, not a shepherd."

To celebrate this great victory, the people of Israel had a party. They sang and danced, and played their tambourines. This victory proved God was with them. With David's help, they had defeated the mighty Philistines!

THE END

TEST YOUR KNOWLEDGE!

(Match the question with the answer at the bottom of the page)

QUESTIONS

What was the name of David's father? ....

Which prophet anointed David as the next king of Israel? ....

Where was King Saul's palace? ....

What musical instrument did David play for King Saul? ....

Where did the Israelites and Philistines set up camp? ....

How tall was Goliath? ....

Who gave David permission to fight Goliath? ....

How many stones did David pick out of the stream? ....

How did David defeat Goliath? ....

In which book of the Bible do we read about David and Goliath? ....

ANSWERS

1. Jesse
2. Samuel
3. Gibeah
4. Harp / lyre
5. Elah Valley
6. 9 feet 9 inches
7. King Saul
8. Five stones
9. With a stone from his sling
10. 1 Samuel 15-18

Complete the Word Search Puzzle

DAVID
GOLIATH
SAMUEL
SAUL
SLING

STONE
GIANT
BETHLEHEM
ISRAELITES
KING

```
S W T W V R L S D B
G A G X J E T T A E
I E M K I N G O V T
A S X U N S O N I H
N I L M E K A E D L
T T G I I L M U O E
X F V K N W U I L H
V E V R K G P W U E
G O L I A T H U B M
I S R A E L I T E S
```

Bible Pathway Adventures®

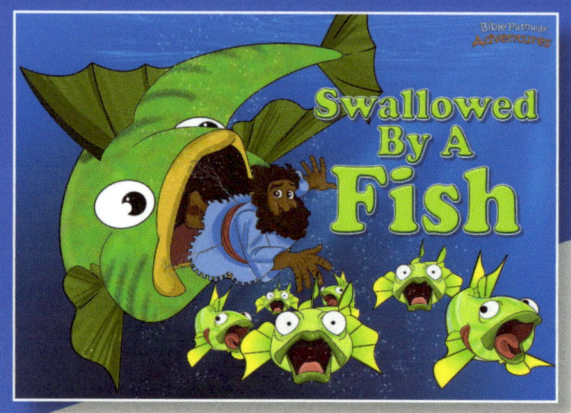
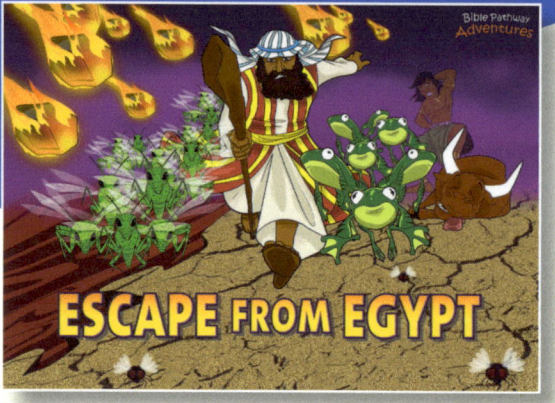

Swallowed by a Fish
The Risen King
Saved by a Donkey
Thrown to the Lions
Witch of Endor
Sold into Slavery
The Great Flood
The Chosen Bride
Shipwrecked!
The Exodus
Escape from Egypt
Birth of the King
Betrayal of the King

Discover more Bible Pathway Adventures' Bible stories!

Check out Bible Pathway Adventures' Activity Books

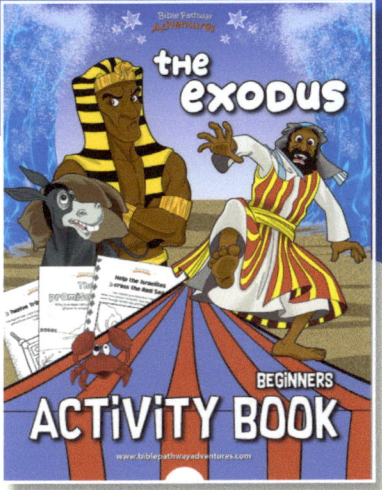
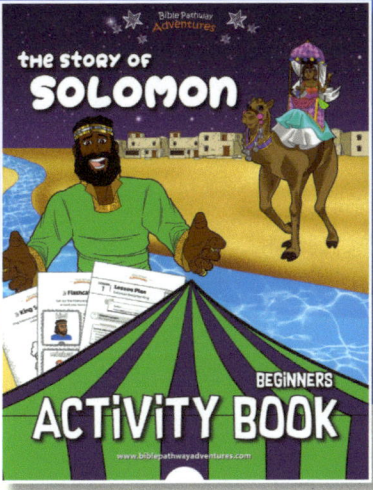
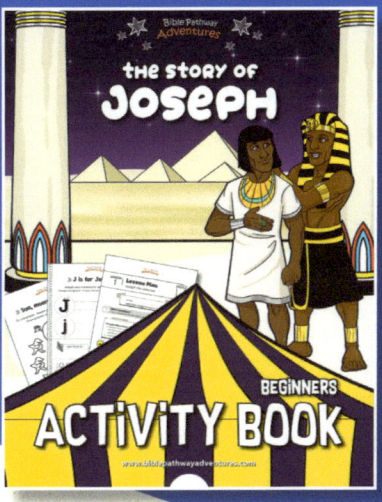

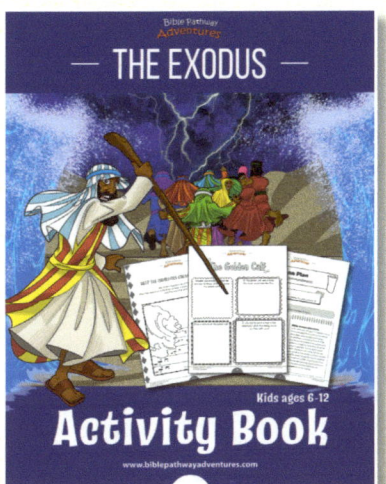

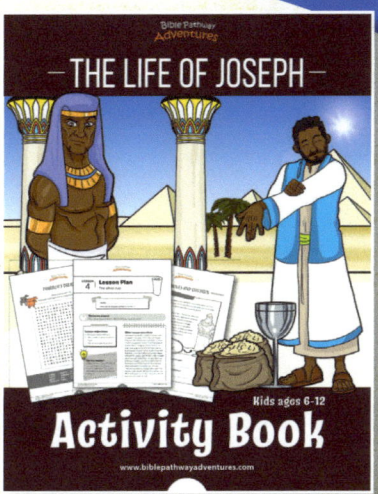

GO TO
www.biblepathwayadventures.com

www.ingramcontent.com/pod-product-compliance
Lightning Source LLC
Chambersburg PA
CBHW041323290426

44108CB00004B/114